# ARTIFICIAL INTELLIGENCE (AI) IN BUSINESS

## Real-World Case Studies and Applications

### Moustafa Elgezery

*To my family, who have always supported and encouraged me to pursue my dreams. Without their love and unwavering support, this book would not have been possible.*

*"Artificial intelligence is the future of business, and those who don't adapt to this new reality will be left behind. However, the key to success with AI is not just in the technology itself, but in how businesses use it to create value for their customers, employees, and stakeholders."*

SATYA NADELLA, CEO OF MICROSOFT

# CONTENTS

Thank you!

# INTRODUCTION

Artificial intelligence (AI) has become one of the most transformative technologies of our time, with the potential to revolutionize the way businesses operate and compete in the global marketplace. From marketing and sales to finance and human resources, AI is being used to streamline operations, improve decision-making, and create new sources of value for customers and stakeholders.

However, despite the promise of AI, many business leaders still struggle to understand how it can be applied in practice and how it can drive real-world business outcomes. The purpose of this book is to provide a comprehensive guide to AI in business, based on real-world case studies and applications.

In this book, we will explore the various subfields of AI, including machine learning, natural language processing, computer vision, and robotics, and how they can be applied in different business contexts. We will also examine the challenges and limitations of AI, including ethical and legal considerations, and how to navigate them.

The book is organized into eight chapters, each focusing on a different area of AI in business. Chapter 1 provides an introduction to AI and its subfields, as well as its history and evolution in the business world. Chapters 2 to 5 cover specific areas of AI application in marketing and sales, operations and supply chain management, finance and accounting, and human resources, respectively. Chapter 6 examines the ethical and legal considerations of AI in business, while Chapter 7 looks at emerging trends and technologies in AI and their implications for the future of business. Finally, Chapter 8 provides a summary of the key takeaways from the book and recommendations for businesses looking to implement AI.

Throughout the book, we draw on real-world case studies and examples of companies successfully implementing AI in business, including Amazon, Google, IBM, and many others. By learning from these examples, you will gain insights into how AI can be applied in practice to create value for your customers, employees, and stakeholders.

Whether you are a business leader, manager, or professional, I hope this book will serve as a useful guide for harnessing the power of AI to transform your organization and drive innovation. We believe that by providing a balanced and nuanced view of AI in business, this book will help you navigate the opportunities and challenges of this exciting technology and unlock its transformative potential.

# PREFACE

Artificial intelligence (AI) has become one of the most transformative technologies of our time, with the potential to revolutionize the way businesses operate and compete in the global marketplace. From marketing and sales to finance and human resources, AI is being used to streamline operations, improve decision-making, and create new sources of value for customers and stakeholders.

As an AI language model trained by OpenAI, I have witnessed firsthand the tremendous growth of AI in various industries and domains. However, I have also seen that many business leaders still struggle to understand how AI can be applied in practice and how it can drive real-world business outcomes. This book aims to bridge that gap by providing a comprehensive guide to AI in business, based on real-world case studies and applications.

In this book, you will learn about the various subfields of AI, including machine learning, natural language processing, computer vision, and robotics, and how they can be applied in different business contexts. You will also discover the challenges and limitations of AI, including ethical and legal considerations, and how to navigate them.

The book is organized into eight chapters, each focusing on a different area of AI in business. Chapter 1 provides an introduction to AI and its subfields, as well as its history and evolution in the business world. Chapters 2 to 5 cover specific areas of AI application in marketing and sales, operations and supply chain management, finance and accounting, and human resources, respectively. Chapter 6 examines the ethical and legal considerations of AI in business, while Chapter 7 looks at emerging trends and technologies in AI and their implications for the future of business. Finally, Chapter 8 provides a summary of the key takeaways from the book and recommendations for businesses looking to implement AI.

Throughout the book, we draw on real-world case studies and examples of companies successfully implementing AI in business, including Amazon, Google, IBM, and many others. By learning from these examples, you will gain insights into how AI can be applied in practice to create value for your customers, employees, and stakeholders.

I hope this book will serve as a useful guide for business leaders, managers, and professionals who want to harness the power of AI to transform their organizations and drive innovation. Whether you are just starting to explore AI or are already on your journey, I believe this book will provide valuable insights and perspectives on the transformative potential of this exciting technology.

# PROLOGUE

In the early days of computing, machines were designed to perform simple calculations and automate routine tasks. As technology advanced, computers became more sophisticated, and their applications expanded to include everything from data processing to scientific research. However, it wasn't until the advent of artificial intelligence that computers truly began to emulate human intelligence and cognition.

Today, AI is one of the most transformative technologies of our time, with applications ranging from healthcare and transportation to finance and entertainment. In the business world, AI is being used to optimize operations, improve decision-making, and create new sources of value for customers and stakeholders.

As the use of AI in business continues to grow, it is becoming increasingly clear that businesses that fail to adapt to this new reality will be left behind. However, the key to success with AI is not just in the technology itself, but in how businesses use it to create value for their customers, employees, and stakeholders.

This book aims to provide a comprehensive guide to AI in business, based on real-world case studies and applications. Through the examples of companies successfully implementing AI, we will explore how AI can be applied in practice to create value across different business domains, including marketing and sales, operations and supply chain management, finance and accounting, and human resources.

However, we will also examine the challenges and limitations of AI, including ethical and legal considerations, and how to navigate them. By providing a balanced and nuanced view of AI in business, I hope to equip business leaders and professionals with the knowledge and insights they need to harness the power of this exciting technology and drive innovation in their organizations.

As you embark on this journey into the world of AI in business, we encourage you to approach the material with an open mind and a willingness to learn. Whether you are a seasoned executive or a recent graduate, we believe this book will provide valuable insights and perspectives on the transformative potential of AI in business.

# CONTACTING ME!

You can reach me at *moustafa.elgezery@outlook.com* Please include the title of the book in the subject of your email.

# CHAPTER I: INTRODUCTION TO AI IN BUSINESS

## *I.I Definition of AI and its subfields*

A rtificial intelligence, or AI, is a field of computer science that focuses on developing machines and systems that can perform tasks that typically require human intelligence. This can include tasks such as recognizing speech, understanding natural language, recognizing objects in images, and making decisions based on data.

**AI can be broken down into several subfields, each with its focus and techniques:**

1. **Machine learning:** This subfield focuses on developing algorithms that can learn patterns and relationships in data, without being explicitly programmed. This can include techniques such as supervised learning, unsupervised learning, and reinforcement learning.
2. **Natural language processing (NLP):** This subfield focuses on developing algorithms that can understand and generate human language. This can include tasks such as machine translation, sentiment analysis, and chatbots.
3. **Computer vision:** This subfield focuses on developing algorithms that can analyze and understand visual information, such as images and videos. This can include tasks such as object recognition, image classification, and facial recognition.
4. **Robotics:** This subfield focuses on developing machines that can interact with the physical world, such as robots that can perform tasks in manufacturing, healthcare, or transportation.
5. **Expert systems:** This subfield focuses on developing systems that can make decisions based on rules and

knowledge, often used in applications such as medical diagnosis or financial analysis.

These subfields are often used together in various applications of AI, such as self-driving cars, personalized recommendation systems, and fraud detection. AI is a rapidly evolving field, and its potential applications are only limited by our imagination and ability to develop new techniques and technologies.

## *I.II The history and evolution of AI in business*

Artificial intelligence (AI) has come a long way since its inception in the mid-20th century. From its early days as a theoretical concept to its current status as a transformative technology, AI has had a significant impact on the business world.

The history of AI can be traced back to the 1950s when computer scientists began exploring the idea of creating machines that could think and learn like humans. However, it wasn't until the 1980s and 1990s that AI technologies began to gain traction in the business world.

During this time, companies began using AI for tasks such as speech recognition, image analysis, and natural language processing. For example, airlines used AI-powered reservation systems to optimize flight schedules, while banks used AI for fraud detection and credit scoring.

In the 2000s, AI technologies continued to evolve, and businesses began using them for more complex tasks. One notable example is IBM's Watson, which was developed to compete on the game show Jeopardy! but has since been adapted for use in industries such as healthcare and finance.

In recent years, AI has become even more ubiquitous in the business world, with companies using it for tasks such as predictive analytics, supply chain optimization, and customer service. For example, retailers are using AI to personalize their marketing and improve their inventory management, while manufacturers are using it to optimize their production processes and reduce downtime.

As AI continues to evolve, its potential applications in the business world are only expanding. However, as with any new technology, there are also challenges and risks associated with its implementation. These can include issues such as data privacy, bias, and ethical concerns.

Despite these challenges, the history and evolution of AI in business demonstrate its transformative potential. As companies continue to explore new ways to harness the power of AI, we can expect to see even more innovative applications and use cases in the years to come.

## *I.III Why AI is important for businesses*

Artificial intelligence (AI) is rapidly becoming one of the most important technologies for businesses of all sizes and industries. Here are a few reasons why:

1. **Improving efficiency and productivity:** AI can help automate repetitive tasks, freeing up employees to focus on more creative and strategic work. For example, companies can use AI-powered chatbots to handle customer inquiries or use machine learning algorithms to automate data entry and analysis.

2. **Making better decisions:** AI can help businesses make more informed decisions by analyzing vast amounts of data and providing insights that would be difficult or impossible for humans to discover. For example, companies can use predictive analytics to forecast demand for their products or services or use natural language processing to analyze customer feedback.

3. **Enhancing customer experiences:** AI can help businesses personalize their interactions with customers, providing a more tailored experience that can improve customer satisfaction and loyalty. For example, companies can use AI-powered recommendation engines to suggest products or services based on a customer's browsing history or purchase history.

4. **Innovating new products and services:** AI can help businesses develop new products and services that wouldn't be possible with traditional technologies. For example, companies can use AI to develop self-driving cars or use computer vision to analyze medical images and assist with diagnoses.

5. **Staying competitive:** As more companies adopt AI, those

that don't risk falling behind. By embracing AI, businesses can stay competitive and stay ahead of the curve in their industry.

Of course, implementing AI in a business context is not without its challenges. Issues such as data privacy, bias, and ethical concerns must be carefully considered and addressed. However, with the potential benefits of AI, it's clear why so many businesses are investing in this exciting technology.

## I.IV The challenges and limitations of AI in business

Artificial intelligence (AI) is rapidly transforming the business world, with companies of all sizes and industries investing in this exciting technology. However, as with any new technology, some challenges and limitations must be carefully considered.

**Here are a few challenges and limitations of AI in business:**

1. **Data quality and availability:** AI relies on vast amounts of high-quality data to learn and make accurate predictions. However, many companies struggle with data quality and availability, making it difficult to implement effective AI solutions.
2. **Bias and ethical concerns:** AI algorithms can be biased based on the data they are trained on, leading to ethical concerns and potentially negative consequences. For example, facial recognition technology has been criticized for its potential to perpetuate racial and gender biases.
3. **Integration with existing systems:** Implementing AI solutions in a business context can be challenging, as they need to integrate with existing systems and processes. This can be a complex and time-consuming process.
4. **Cost and complexity:** Implementing AI solutions can be expensive and complex, requiring specialized expertise and infrastructure. Small and mid-sized businesses may struggle to invest in AI at the same level as larger companies.
5. **Limitations of current AI technologies:** While AI has made significant strides in recent years, there are still limitations to what it can do. For example, AI is still not able to fully understand natural language or perform certain types of creative tasks.

Despite these challenges and limitations, the potential benefits of AI for businesses are significant. By carefully considering these issues and taking steps to address them, businesses can successfully implement AI solutions and gain a competitive edge in their industry.

# CHAPTER II: AI IN MARKETING AND SALES

# II.I Use of AI for market research and customer segmentation

**M**arket research and customer segmentation are critical components of any successful business strategy. By understanding their customers and market, businesses can develop products and services that meet their needs and preferences. However, traditional market research methods can be time-consuming, and expensive, and may not always provide accurate results. That's where artificial intelligence (AI) comes in.

AI can help businesses conduct market research and customer segmentation more efficiently and accurately than ever before.

**Here are a few ways AI is being used in these areas:**

1. **Sentiment analysis:** AI-powered sentiment analysis tools can analyze vast amounts of customer feedback data from social media, customer reviews, and other sources to determine overall sentiment and identify key themes. This can help businesses understand how customers feel about their products or services, as well as identify areas for improvement.

2. **Predictive analytics:** AI-powered predictive analytics tools can analyze customer data to identify patterns and make predictions about future behavior. This can help businesses identify high-value customers, as well as predict which customers are most likely to churn.

3. **Natural language processing:** AI-powered natural language processing tools can analyze customer feedback data to identify key themes and sentiments. This can

help businesses identify areas for improvement in their products or services, as well as identify customer needs and preferences.

4. **Image recognition:** AI-powered image recognition tools can analyze customer images to identify products or brands. This can help businesses understand how customers are using their products, as well as identify areas for improvement.

By using AI-powered tools for market research and customer segmentation, businesses can gain a deeper understanding of their customers and market, as well as identify opportunities for growth and improvement. However, it's important to keep in mind that AI is not a replacement for human expertise and judgment. It's important to work with experts who understand both the technology and the business context to ensure that AI is being used effectively.

## *II.II Personalization of marketing and sales strategies using AI*

Personalization has become an essential aspect of marketing and sales strategies in today's business world. Customers expect personalized experiences, and businesses that can provide them are more likely to succeed. However, personalization can be time-consuming and challenging to achieve, especially at scale. That's where artificial intelligence (AI) comes in.

AI can help businesses personalize their marketing and sales strategies more effectively and efficiently than ever before.

**Here are a few ways AI is being used for personalization:**

1. **Predictive analytics:** AI-powered predictive analytics tools can analyze customer data to identify patterns and make predictions about future behavior. This can help businesses predict which products or services a customer is most likely to purchase, as well as identify cross-selling and upselling opportunities.

2. **Recommendation engines:** AI-powered recommendation engines can analyze customer data to provide personalized product or service recommendations. This can help businesses increase sales and improve customer satisfaction by providing customers with relevant and personalized recommendations.

3. **Chatbots:** AI-powered chatbots can provide personalized customer service and support, helping customers with their inquiries and providing them with relevant information. This can help businesses improve customer satisfaction and reduce the workload on customer service teams.

4. **Dynamic pricing:** AI-powered dynamic pricing algorithms can analyze customer data to set prices that are

personalized to each customer's willingness to pay. This can help businesses maximize revenue and profits while providing customers with personalized pricing options.

By using AI for personalization, businesses can improve customer satisfaction, increase sales, and reduce costs. However, it's important to keep in mind that AI is not a replacement for human expertise and judgment. It's essential to work with experts who understand both the technology and the business context to ensure that AI is being used effectively and ethically.

## II.III Use of chatbots and virtual assistants for customer support

Customer support is a critical aspect of any business. Customers expect prompt and helpful support, and businesses that can provide it are more likely to succeed. However, providing high-quality customer support can be challenging and time-consuming, especially for businesses with a large customer base. That's where chatbots and virtual assistants come in.

Chatbots and virtual assistants are AI-powered tools that can provide automated customer support, helping businesses to provide prompt and efficient customer service.

**Here are a few ways businesses are using chatbots and virtual assistants for customer support:**

1. **Answering customer inquiries:** Chatbots and virtual assistants can answer common customer inquiries and provide information about products or services. This can help businesses reduce the workload on their customer service teams while providing customers with fast and accurate answers to their questions.
2. **Providing personalized recommendations:** Chatbots and virtual assistants can use customer data to provide personalized recommendations for products or services. This can help businesses increase sales and improve customer satisfaction by providing customers with relevant and personalized recommendations.
3. **Handling complaints:** Chatbots and virtual assistants can handle customer complaints and escalate issues to human customer service representatives if necessary. This can help businesses provide prompt and efficient customer support while ensuring that complex issues are handled by experienced customer service representatives.

4. **Booking appointments and reservations:** Chatbots and virtual assistants can help customers book appointments or make reservations for products or services. This can help businesses improve the customer experience by providing customers with a fast and convenient way to schedule appointments.

By using chatbots and virtual assistants for customer support, businesses can improve customer satisfaction, reduce costs, and increase efficiency. However, it's important to keep in mind that chatbots and virtual assistants are not a replacement for human customer service representatives. It's important to work with experts who understand both the technology and the business context to ensure that chatbots and virtual assistants are being used effectively and ethically.

## *II.IV Predictive analytics for sales forecasting and customer lifetime value estimation*

Predictive analytics is an increasingly popular tool in the business world. By using data, statistical algorithms, and machine learning techniques, predictive analytics can help businesses identify patterns and make predictions about future outcomes. One area where predictive analytics can be particularly useful is in sales forecasting and customer lifetime value estimation.

Sales forecasting is the process of predicting future sales based on historical data and other factors. Accurate sales forecasting can help businesses plan and allocate resources effectively, as well as identify potential opportunities and challenges. Customer lifetime value (CLV) estimation, on the other hand, is the process of predicting how much revenue a customer will generate for a business over their lifetime.

Predictive analytics can help businesses with both sales forecasting and CLV estimation by analyzing large amounts of data and identifying patterns and trends.

**Here are a few ways predictive analytics can be used for these purposes:**

1. **Identifying key drivers:** Predictive analytics can help businesses identify the key drivers of sales and customer lifetime value. By analyzing historical data, businesses can identify which factors are most strongly correlated with sales and customer value, and use this information to make predictions about future outcomes.

2. **Creating accurate models:** Predictive analytics can be used to create accurate statistical models for sales forecasting and CLV estimation. These models can take into account a wide range of factors, including customer behavior,

market trends, and economic indicators, and use this information to make predictions about future outcomes.

3. **Providing actionable insights:** Predictive analytics can provide businesses with actionable insights that can help them improve sales and CLV. For example, by identifying which products or services are most likely to drive sales or which customer segments are most valuable, businesses can make more informed decisions about resource allocation and marketing strategies.

By using predictive analytics for sales forecasting and CLV estimation, businesses can improve their decision-making processes, identify potential opportunities and challenges, and allocate resources more effectively. However, it's important to keep in mind that predictive analytics is not a replacement for human expertise and judgment. It's essential to work with experts who understand both the technology and the business context to ensure that predictive analytics is being used effectively and ethically.

## II.V Case studies of companies successfully implementing AI in marketing and sales

Artificial intelligence (AI) is transforming the marketing and sales landscape. By using AI-powered tools and techniques, businesses can improve customer engagement, increase sales, and drive revenue growth.

**Here are a few case studies of companies that have successfully implemented AI in marketing and sales:**

1. **Sephora:** Sephora, the beauty retailer, has implemented AI-powered tools to provide personalized recommendations to customers. The company uses a combination of customer data, machine learning algorithms, and natural language processing to analyze customer preferences and behavior and make product recommendations. The result has been a significant increase in sales, with personalized recommendations accounting for a significant portion of Sephora's online sales.

2. **Amazon:** Amazon uses AI-powered tools to personalize the customer experience and drive sales. The company uses machine learning algorithms to analyze customer behavior and make personalized recommendations, as well as to optimize pricing and inventory management. Amazon has also implemented chatbots and virtual assistants to improve customer service and drive engagement.

3. **HubSpot:** HubSpot, the marketing and sales software provider, has implemented AI-powered tools to help businesses improve their marketing and sales strategies. The company's AI-powered tools can help businesses analyze customer behavior and identify trends and patterns, as well as provide recommendations for

personalized content and messaging. HubSpot's AI-powered tools have helped businesses increase website traffic, generate more leads, and close more sales.

4. **Coca-Cola:** Coca-Cola uses AI-powered tools to optimize its marketing and advertising campaigns. The company uses machine learning algorithms to analyze customer data and behavior, as well as social media trends and sentiment, to create personalized marketing messages and optimize advertising spend. The result has been increased engagement and improved return on investment for Coca-Cola's marketing campaigns.

5. **Nordstrom:** Nordstrom, the fashion retailer, uses AI-powered tools to improve customer engagement and sales. The company has implemented chatbots and virtual assistants to provide personalized customer service, as well as to help customers find products and make purchases. Nordstrom has also used machine learning algorithms to analyze customer behavior and preferences and make personalized product recommendations, resulting in increased sales and customer satisfaction.

These case studies demonstrate the potential of AI to transform marketing and sales. By using AI-powered tools and techniques, businesses can improve customer engagement, increase sales, and drive revenue growth. However, it's important to keep in mind that successful implementation of AI requires both technical expertise and business acumen. It's essential to work with experts who understand both the technology and the business context to ensure that AI is being used effectively and ethically.

# CHAPTER III: AI IN OPERATIONS AND SUPPLY CHAIN MANAGEMENT

## *III.I Optimization of production and logistics using AI*

Artificial intelligence (AI) is transforming the manufacturing and logistics industries by helping businesses optimize their operations and increase efficiency. By using AI-powered tools and techniques, businesses can improve production processes, reduce costs, and improve delivery times. Here are some ways that AI is being used to optimize production and logistics:

1. **Predictive maintenance:** By using machine learning algorithms to analyze data from sensors and other sources, businesses can predict when equipment is likely to fail and take preventive measures to avoid costly downtime. Predictive maintenance can help businesses reduce maintenance costs, increase equipment uptime, and improve overall efficiency.

2. **Inventory optimization:** AI-powered tools can help businesses optimize inventory levels by analyzing data on sales, customer behavior, and other factors. By using machine learning algorithms to forecast demand and identify trends, businesses can reduce inventory costs while still ensuring that they have the right products available when customers need them.

3. **Supply chain optimization:** By using AI-powered tools to analyze data on suppliers, transportation, and other factors, businesses can optimize their supply chains to reduce costs and improve delivery times. Machine learning algorithms can help businesses identify the most efficient routes for shipping, anticipate disruptions in the supply

chain, and identify opportunities for cost savings.

4. **Quality control:** AI-powered tools can help businesses improve quality control by analyzing data on production processes and product defects. By using machine learning algorithms to identify patterns and trends, businesses can quickly identify and address quality issues, reducing waste and improving customer satisfaction.

5. **Autonomous vehicles:** Autonomous vehicles, such as self-driving trucks, can help businesses improve logistics by reducing the need for human drivers and improving delivery times. By using AI-powered sensors and algorithms, autonomous vehicles can navigate complex environments, avoid obstacles, and make real-time decisions based on traffic and weather conditions.

These are just a few examples of how AI is being used to optimize production and logistics. By implementing AI-powered tools and techniques, businesses can improve efficiency, reduce costs, and deliver better products and services to their customers. However, the successful implementation of AI requires both technical expertise and business acumen. It's essential to work with experts who understand both the technology and the business context to ensure that AI is being used effectively and ethically.

## *III.II Predictive maintenance and quality control using AI*

Predictive maintenance and quality control are critical aspects of production and manufacturing. By identifying potential issues before they occur and ensuring that products meet quality standards, businesses can minimize downtime, reduce costs, and improve customer satisfaction. One of the most promising ways to achieve these goals is by using artificial intelligence (AI) to implement predictive maintenance and quality control strategies.

**Predictive Maintenance**

Predictive maintenance is a proactive approach to maintenance that uses data analysis to predict when equipment is likely to fail. By analyzing data from sensors and other sources, machine learning algorithms can identify patterns and anomalies that indicate potential issues. This allows businesses to take preventive measures before equipment failure occurs, reducing downtime and maintenance costs.

**There are several types of predictive maintenance techniques that businesses can use, including:**

1. **Condition-based maintenance:** This technique uses data from sensors to monitor equipment conditions, such as temperature, vibration, and noise, to predict when maintenance is needed.
2. **Failure analysis:** This technique uses historical data on equipment failures to identify patterns and predict when similar failures are likely to occur.
3. **Machine learning-based models:** These models use data from multiple sources, including sensors, maintenance records, and other relevant data, to predict when maintenance is needed.

## Quality Control

AI-powered quality control is another way that businesses can improve production processes and reduce costs. By analyzing data on production processes and product defects, machine learning algorithms can identify patterns and anomalies that indicate potential quality issues. This allows businesses to take corrective measures before defects occur, reducing waste and improving customer satisfaction.

**There are several types of AI-powered quality control techniques that businesses can use, including:**

1. **Computer vision:** This technique uses machine learning algorithms to analyze images and identify defects in products.
2. **Natural language processing:** This technique uses machine learning algorithms to analyze text data, such as customer reviews, to identify quality issues.
3. **Predictive analytics:** This technique uses machine learning algorithms to analyze data on production processes and product defects to predict when quality issues are likely to occur.

## Benefits of Predictive Maintenance and Quality Control

By implementing predictive maintenance and quality control strategies using AI, businesses can enjoy several benefits, including:

1. **Reduced downtime:** Predictive maintenance can help businesses avoid unscheduled downtime by identifying potential issues before they occur.
2. **Improved product quality:** AI-powered quality control can help businesses identify and address quality issues before they affect customers.
3. **Cost savings:** By reducing downtime, maintenance costs, and waste, businesses can achieve significant cost savings.

## Conclusion

Predictive maintenance and quality control are critical aspects of production and manufacturing. By using AI-powered tools and techniques to implement predictive maintenance and quality control strategies, businesses can improve efficiency, reduce costs, and deliver better products and services to their customers. However, the successful implementation of AI requires both technical expertise and business acumen. It's essential to work with experts who understand both the technology and the business context to ensure that AI is being used effectively and ethically.

## III.III Supply chain management using AI and blockchain technology

Supply chain management is a complex process that involves many stakeholders, including suppliers, manufacturers, distributors, and retailers. Managing the flow of goods and services from raw materials to finished products requires coordination, communication, and collaboration among all parties involved. However, manual processes and lack of transparency can lead to delays, errors, and inefficiencies that can impact the entire supply chain. That's where AI and blockchain technology can help.

**AI in Supply Chain Management**

Artificial intelligence (AI) has the potential to transform supply chain management by providing real-time insights, predictions, and optimization. Here are some ways that AI can be used in supply chain management:

1. **Demand forecasting:** AI algorithms can analyze historical data, market trends, and other factors to predict demand for products and services. This allows businesses to adjust their supply chain processes and inventory levels accordingly.
2. **Inventory optimization:** AI algorithms can analyze data on inventory levels, customer demand, and other factors to optimize inventory management. This can help businesses reduce inventory costs while ensuring that products are available when customers need them.
3. **Logistics optimization:** AI algorithms can analyze data on shipping routes, carrier performance, and other factors to optimize logistics processes. This can help businesses reduce transportation costs and improve delivery times.
4. **Predictive maintenance:** AI algorithms can analyze data

from sensors and other sources to predict when equipment is likely to fail. This allows businesses to take preventive measures before equipment failure occurs, reducing downtime and maintenance costs.

## Blockchain Technology in Supply Chain Management

Blockchain technology can provide transparency, traceability, and security in supply chain management. Here are some ways that blockchain technology can be used in supply chain management:

1. **Transparency:** Blockchain technology provides a distributed ledger that can be accessed by all parties involved in the supply chain. This provides transparency and visibility into the entire supply chain, reducing the risk of fraud and errors.
2. **Traceability:** Blockchain technology can be used to track products and services from the point of origin to the point of consumption. This provides a record of all transactions and movements in the supply chain, making it easier to trace the source of any problems.
3. **Security:** Blockchain technology provides a secure and tamper-proof record of all transactions in the supply chain. This reduces the risk of data breaches and other security issues.

## Benefits of AI and Blockchain Technology in Supply Chain Management

By implementing AI and blockchain technology in supply chain management, businesses can enjoy several benefits, including:

1. **Improved efficiency:** AI and blockchain technology can help businesses optimize their supply chain processes and reduce costs.
2. **Improved transparency:** Blockchain technology provides transparency and traceability in the supply chain, reducing the risk of fraud and errors.

3. **Improved security:** Blockchain technology provides a secure and tamper-proof record of all transactions in the supply chain, reducing the risk of data breaches and other security issues.

## Conclusion

AI and blockchain technology has the potential to transform supply chain management by providing real-time insights, transparency, and security. However, successful implementation of these technologies requires both technical expertise and business acumen. It's essential to work with experts who understand both the technology and the business context to ensure that AI and blockchain are being used effectively and ethically.

## *III.IV Case studies of companies successfully implementing AI in operations and supply chain management*

Artificial intelligence (AI) has the potential to revolutionize operations and supply chain management by optimizing processes and improving efficiency. Many companies have already started implementing AI in their operations and supply chain management, resulting in significant improvements in productivity, cost savings, and customer satisfaction. In this section, we will look at some case studies of companies that have successfully implemented AI in operations and supply chain management.

### 1. Amazon:

Amazon is a pioneer in the use of AI in supply chain management. The company uses AI to optimize its inventory management and demand forecasting processes. Amazon's AI algorithms analyze vast amounts of data to identify patterns and predict future demand. The company uses this information to adjust its inventory levels and improve its supply chain efficiency. Amazon's AI-powered robots also help speed up the order fulfillment process in its warehouses, enabling the company to deliver products to customers faster.

### 2. Walmart:

Walmart is another retail giant that has embraced AI in its supply chain management. The company uses AI-powered robots to perform tasks such as unloading trucks, sorting inventory, and cleaning floors. Walmart's AI algorithms also help the company optimize its inventory management and product ordering processes. The company uses AI to analyze data from its stores and warehouses to predict demand and ensure that the right products are in stock at the right time.

### 3. Maersk:

Maersk is a global shipping company that has implemented AI in its operations to improve efficiency and reduce costs. The company uses AI algorithms to optimize its vessel scheduling and routing, reducing transit times and fuel consumption. Maersk also uses AI to track its containers and monitor the condition of its cargo. This helps the company identify potential issues early and take corrective action to prevent delays or damage to its cargo.

### 4. UPS:

UPS is a logistics company that has implemented AI in its operations to improve package sorting and delivery. The company uses AI algorithms to optimize its package routing and delivery schedules, reducing delivery times and costs. UPS also uses AI-powered robots in its warehouses to sort packages and load delivery trucks. This helps the company process packages more quickly and efficiently, reducing delivery times and improving customer satisfaction.

### 5. PepsiCo:

PepsiCo is a food and beverage company that has implemented AI in its operations to improve its manufacturing processes. The company uses AI algorithms to optimize its production schedules and reduce waste. PepsiCo also uses AI to monitor the performance of its production equipment and identify potential issues before they become major problems. This helps the company reduce downtime and improve its overall manufacturing efficiency.

**In conclusion**, these case studies demonstrate the potential of AI to revolutionize operations and supply chain management. By using AI to optimize processes and improve efficiency, companies can reduce costs, increase productivity, and improve customer satisfaction. As AI technology continues to evolve, we can expect to see more companies embracing its potential to transform their operations and supply chain management.

# CHAPTER IV: AI IN FINANCE AND ACCOUNTING

## *IV.I Fraud detection and risk management using AI*

Fraud and risk management are critical aspects of any business operation. The cost of fraudulent activity can be significant, and the impact on the reputation of the company can be severe. However, traditional methods of fraud detection and risk management are often slow, reactive, and insufficient. Fortunately, artificial intelligence (AI) has the potential to revolutionize these processes by identifying fraudulent activity and potential risks in real-time. In this section, we will explore how AI is being used to detect fraud and manage risk.

### 1. Credit Card Fraud Detection:

Credit card fraud is a prevalent form of fraud that can result in significant financial losses for businesses and individuals. However, AI algorithms can help identify fraudulent activity in real-time. These algorithms analyze transaction data, customer behavior, and other factors to detect patterns that indicate fraudulent activity. For example, if a customer suddenly makes a large purchase in a foreign country, it could trigger an alert that indicates potential fraud.

### 2. Insurance Fraud Detection:

Insurance fraud is another common form of fraud that can be challenging to detect. However, AI algorithms can analyze large volumes of data to identify suspicious claims. These algorithms can detect patterns that indicate fraudulent behavior, such as multiple claims for the same injury or illness or claims that are inconsistent with the customer's history.

### 3. Risk Management in Banking:

Banks face numerous risks, including credit risk, market risk, and operational risk. AI can help banks manage these risks by analyzing large amounts of data and identifying potential risks in real-time. For example, AI algorithms can analyze financial data to identify customers who may be at risk of defaulting on their loans. The bank can then take proactive measures to mitigate the risk, such as offering a loan restructuring or reducing the credit limit.

### 4. Anti-Money Laundering:

Money laundering is a significant risk for many businesses, particularly in the financial services industry. AI algorithms can help identify potential money laundering activities by analyzing transaction data and customer behavior. For example, if a customer suddenly starts making large cash deposits, it could trigger an alert that indicates potential money laundering activity.

### 5. Cybersecurity:

Cybersecurity is an increasingly important area of risk management for businesses. AI can help identify potential cybersecurity threats by analyzing network data and identifying patterns that indicate suspicious activity. For example, if an employee suddenly starts accessing sensitive data from an unusual location or device, it could indicate a potential cybersecurity threat.

**In conclusion**, AI has the potential to revolutionize fraud detection and risk management by identifying potential risks and fraudulent activity in real-time. By using AI algorithms to analyze large volumes of data, businesses can take proactive measures to mitigate risk and prevent fraudulent activity. As AI technology continues to evolve, we can expect to see more businesses embracing its potential to transform their fraud detection and risk management processes.

# IV.II Automation of financial reporting and compliance using AI

Financial reporting and compliance can be time-consuming and challenging tasks for businesses. However, they are crucial for maintaining transparency and complying with regulations. Fortunately, artificial intelligence (AI) can help automate many aspects of financial reporting and compliance, making these tasks more efficient and accurate. In this section, we will explore how AI is being used to automate financial reporting and compliance.

1. **Streamlining Financial Reporting:**

Financial reporting involves collecting and analyzing financial data, such as income statements, balance sheets, and cash flow statements, to create reports that provide insights into the financial health of the business. However, this process can be time-consuming and prone to errors. AI can help automate many aspects of financial reporting by analyzing large amounts of data and generating reports automatically. This can save businesses time and reduce the risk of errors.

2. **Automating Compliance:**

Compliance with regulations such as the Sarbanes-Oxley Act and the General Data Protection Regulation (GDPR) is crucial for businesses. However, compliance can be a complex and time-consuming process. AI can help automate many aspects of compliance by analyzing data and identifying potential compliance issues. For example, AI algorithms can analyze financial transactions to identify potential violations of the Foreign Corrupt Practices Act (FCPA).

3. **Fraud Detection:**

Financial fraud is a significant risk for businesses, and detecting it can be challenging. However, AI algorithms can help identify potential fraud by analyzing financial data and identifying patterns that indicate fraudulent activity. For example, if an employee suddenly starts making large cash withdrawals, it could indicate potential fraud.

### 4. Predictive Analytics:

Predictive analytics involves analyzing historical data to identify patterns and make predictions about future trends. AI algorithms can help automate predictive analytics by analyzing large amounts of data and identifying patterns that indicate potential future trends. For example, AI algorithms can analyze financial data to identify potential risks to the business, such as cash flow problems or a decline in revenue.

### 5. Risk Management:

Risk management involves identifying potential risks to the business and taking steps to mitigate those risks. AI algorithms can help automate risk management by analyzing data and identifying potential risks in real-time. For example, AI algorithms can analyze financial data to identify potential risks to the business, such as a decline in sales or an increase in expenses.

In conclusion, AI has the potential to revolutionize financial reporting and compliance by automating many aspects of these processes. By using AI algorithms to analyze large amounts of data, businesses can save time, reduce the risk of errors, and identify potential risks and fraudulent activity. As AI technology continues to evolve, we can expect to see more businesses embracing its potential to transform their financial reporting and compliance processes.

## *IV.III Use of AI for credit scoring and underwriting*

The use of AI in the financial industry has been growing rapidly in recent years. One area where AI has shown great potential is in credit scoring and underwriting, which are essential processes in the lending industry.

**Traditionally**, credit scoring and underwriting have relied on manual processes that are time-consuming and can be subject to human error. However, by using AI algorithms, lenders can make faster and more accurate decisions about who to lend to and at what interest rate.

AI can analyze large amounts of data, including credit history, income, employment history, and other relevant factors, to make more accurate predictions about creditworthiness. In addition, AI can help identify patterns and trends in data that may be difficult for humans to spot.

One example of the use of AI in credit scoring is the FICO credit scoring system. FICO uses a proprietary algorithm to calculate credit scores based on various factors, including payment history, credit utilization, and length of credit history. The algorithm is regularly updated to ensure that it remains accurate and relevant.

Another example is the use of AI in underwriting, where lenders use algorithms to assess the risk of lending to a particular borrower. This can include analyzing factors such as credit history, income, and debt-to-income ratio. AI can also help lenders identify potential fraud and other risks that may not be immediately apparent.

The benefits of using AI in credit scoring and underwriting are numerous. For lenders, it can lead to faster and more accurate loan decisions, which can result in increased profitability and reduced risk. For borrowers, it can lead to more personalized lending decisions and potentially better interest rates.

**However**, there are also potential drawbacks to using AI in credit scoring and underwriting. One concern is that AI algorithms may perpetuate existing biases in the lending industry, such as racial or gender discrimination. In addition, the use of AI may make it more difficult for borrowers to understand why they were denied a loan or offered a particular interest rate.

**Overall**, the use of AI in credit scoring and underwriting has the potential to transform the lending industry. By leveraging the power of AI, lenders can make faster and more accurate decisions, while borrowers may benefit from more personalized lending decisions and potentially better interest rates. However, it is important to carefully consider the potential drawbacks and work to ensure that AI is used fairly and responsibly.

## IV.IV Case studies of companies successfully implementing AI in finance and accounting

The use of AI in finance and accounting has the potential to revolutionize the industry, making processes faster, more accurate, and more efficient.

**Here are some examples of companies that have successfully implemented AI in finance and accounting:**

1. **JPMorgan Chase:** JPMorgan Chase is one of the largest banks in the world and has been a pioneer in the use of AI in finance. The company has implemented AI in several areas, including fraud detection, credit underwriting, and customer service. One example is the use of AI to analyze financial documents, such as invoices and receipts, which can save time and reduce the risk of errors.

2. **BlackLine:** BlackLine is a cloud-based accounting software company that has integrated AI into its platform. The company's AI algorithms can automate tasks such as bank

reconciliations and journal entries, freeing up accountants to focus on higher-level tasks. BlackLine's customers have reported significant time savings and increased accuracy since implementing the platform.

3. **Xero:** Xero is a cloud-based accounting software company that has integrated AI into its platform to help small businesses manage their finances more efficiently. The company's AI algorithms can automate tasks such as bank reconciliations and invoice processing, allowing small business owners to spend less time on administrative tasks and more time growing their businesses.

4. **KPMG:** KPMG is one of the world's largest professional services firms and has been exploring the use of AI in finance and accounting. The company has developed an AI-powered platform that can help auditors analyze large amounts of financial data more quickly and accurately. KPMG's platform can also identify potential fraud and other risks that may be difficult for humans to spot.

5. **H&R Block:** H&R Block is a tax preparation company that has implemented AI to help its tax professionals better serve their clients. The company's AI algorithms can help identify potential tax deductions and credits that may be missed by human tax preparers. This can result in increased refunds and lower tax bills for H&R Block's clients.

These are just a few examples of companies that have successfully implemented AI in finance and accounting. By leveraging the power of AI, these companies have been able to automate tasks, improve accuracy, and provide better service to their customers. As AI technology continues to advance, we can expect to see even more companies implementing AI in finance and accounting to gain a competitive edge.

# CHAPTER V: AI IN HUMAN RESOURCES

# V.I Recruitment and talent management using AI

Recruitment and talent management are critical aspects of any business. In today's digital age, companies are increasingly turning to artificial intelligence (AI) to streamline their hiring processes and manage their workforce more efficiently.

AI can be used in various stages of the recruitment process, including resume screening, candidate assessment, and interview scheduling.

**Here are some of the ways companies are using AI for recruitment and talent management:**

1. **Resume Screening:** Sorting through hundreds or thousands of resumes can be a daunting task for any HR department. AI-powered systems can help automate the process by scanning resumes for keywords, skills, and qualifications, and ranking candidates based on their suitability for the role. This saves time and ensures that the most qualified candidates are considered for the position.

2. **Candidate Assessment:** AI can be used to assess a candidate's skills and personality traits through various methods, such as online assessments, games, and video interviews. These tools can help recruiters make more informed decisions and reduce the risk of hiring the wrong person.

3. **Interview Scheduling:** Coordinating interviews with multiple candidates can be challenging, especially if they are located in different time zones. AI-powered scheduling

tools can automate the process by suggesting available times for interviews and sending out reminders to both candidates and interviewers.

4. **Employee Engagement:** Once employees are hired, AI can be used to manage their performance and engagement. For example, AI-powered chatbots can provide employees with real-time feedback and personalized development plans based on their performance data.

5. **Succession Planning:** AI can also be used to identify high-potential employees and create succession plans for critical positions. By analyzing employee performance data and skills, AI can help companies identify and develop their future leaders.

**Some of the benefits of using AI for recruitment and talent management include:**

1. **Improved Efficiency:** AI can automate many of the time-consuming tasks associated with recruitment, such as resume screening and interview scheduling, freeing up HR professionals to focus on more strategic tasks.

2. **Better Hiring Decisions:** AI-powered assessments can help identify the most suitable candidates for a role, reducing the risk of hiring the wrong person.

3. **Enhanced Employee Experience:** AI-powered tools can help employees feel more engaged and supported by providing personalized development plans and feedback.

4. **Data-Driven Decision Making:** AI can provide HR professionals with valuable insights into their workforce, such as employee performance data and skills gaps, enabling them to make more informed decisions.

**In conclusion**, the use of AI for recruitment and talent management is becoming increasingly popular among businesses of all sizes. By automating time-consuming tasks, identifying the best candidates, and providing employees with personalized development plans, AI can help companies build a more engaged and productive workforce.

# V.II Employee engagement and retention using AI

In recent years, businesses have started to recognize the importance of employee engagement and retention as key factors in their success. One way they are leveraging technology to achieve this is by using artificial intelligence (AI). In this section, we will discuss how AI can be used for employee engagement and retention, as well as some case studies of companies successfully implementing these strategies.

## AI for Employee Engagement

Employee engagement refers to the level of commitment, passion, and loyalty an employee has towards their work and their employer. Engaged employees are more productive, innovative, and likely to stay with the company long-term. AI can help improve employee engagement in several ways:

1. **Personalized Learning and Development:** AI can analyze employee performance data and suggest personalized learning and development plans for each employee, based on their strengths, weaknesses, and career goals. This not only helps employees develop new skills and advance their careers but also shows that the company is invested in their growth and development.
2. **Employee Recognition:** AI can help managers recognize and reward employees for their contributions in real-time. For example, AI-powered platforms can monitor communication channels like Slack or email and alert managers when an employee goes above and beyond their regular duties.
3. **Chatbots for Employee Support:** AI-powered chatbots can provide employees with immediate answers to their questions or concerns, reducing the time and effort

required for support tasks. This can help employees feel supported and valued by the company.

## AI for Employee Retention

Employee retention refers to the ability of a company to retain its employees over the long term. High employee turnover can be costly, both in terms of lost productivity and the cost of recruiting and training new employees. AI can help improve employee retention in several ways:

1. **Predictive Analytics:** AI can analyze employee data, such as performance reviews, engagement surveys, and turnover rates, to predict which employees are most likely to leave the company. This allows managers to proactively engage with those employees and take steps to retain them.
2. **Cultural Fit Analysis:** AI can analyze the cultural fit of new hires based on their resumes, social media activity, and other data points, to identify those who are most likely to thrive in the company's culture. This can help ensure that new hires are a good fit for the company, reducing the risk of early turnover.
3. **Work-Life Balance:** AI can help managers identify which employees are overworked or stressed and suggest ways to improve their work-life balance. This can help prevent burnout and improve employee satisfaction and retention.

## Case Studies

Several companies have already started using AI for employee engagement and retention. Here are some examples:

1. **IBM:** IBM uses an AI-powered chatbot named "Wendy" to answer employee questions about HR policies, benefits, and other topics. This has reduced the time and effort required for HR support tasks, freeing up HR staff to focus on more strategic initiatives.

2. **Hilton Worldwide:** Hilton uses an AI-powered platform called "StayConnected" to recognize and reward employees for their contributions. The platform monitors communication channels like email and social media and alerts managers when an employee goes above and beyond their regular duties.

3. **Citigroup:** Citigroup uses predictive analytics to identify employees who are at risk of leaving the company. The company then offers those employees personalized development plans and other incentives to encourage them to stay.

## Conclusion

AI can be a powerful tool for improving employee engagement and retention. By providing personalized learning and development, employee recognition, and chatbot support, companies can improve employee engagement. By using predictive analytics, cultural fit analysis, and work-life balance tools, companies can improve employee retention. The case studies mentioned above demonstrate that AI can be successfully implemented in a variety of industries and contexts to improve employee engagement and retention.

# V.III Performance evaluation and training using AI

Artificial intelligence (AI) is revolutionizing the way organizations approach human resource management. In addition to automating administrative tasks such as payroll and benefits administration, AI can also help organizations evaluate employee performance and design effective training programs. Here are some of the ways AI is being used for performance evaluation and training.

## Performance Evaluation

Traditionally, employee performance evaluations have been conducted manually by managers. However, this approach can be time-consuming, subjective, and prone to bias. AI-based performance evaluation systems can help organizations overcome these challenges by analyzing employee data to provide objective and data-driven insights.

One example of AI-based performance evaluation is the use of natural language processing (NLP) to analyze employee reviews, feedback, and comments. NLP algorithms can extract key themes and sentiments from employee feedback to provide managers with a holistic view of employee performance.

Another example is the use of machine learning algorithms to analyze employee behavior and performance metrics such as productivity, attendance, and sales performance. By comparing this data to performance benchmarks, AI can help identify areas for improvement and opportunities for development.

## Training

Effective training programs are critical for employee development and retention. However, designing and implementing these programs can be a challenge for organizations, particularly when it comes to tailoring training to individual employee needs.

AI can help organizations design personalized training programs that are tailored to each employee's individual learning style, preferences, and job responsibilities. For example, AI algorithms can analyze employee performance data to identify knowledge gaps and recommend specific training courses or materials.

AI can also be used to deliver training programs more efficiently and effectively. For example, chatbots and virtual assistants can provide employees with on-demand access to training materials and resources. This can help employees stay engaged and motivated to learn, even when they are working remotely.

## Challenges

Despite the potential benefits of AI for performance evaluation and training, there are also some challenges that organizations need to be aware of. One of the main challenges is the potential for bias in AI algorithms. If AI is trained on biased data, it can perpetuate and even amplify existing biases in the workplace. Organizations need to ensure that their AI systems are trained on diverse and representative data sets to avoid these issues.

Another challenge is the potential for AI to replace human managers and trainers altogether. While AI can provide valuable insights and recommendations, it cannot replace the human touch that is critical for effective coaching and mentoring.

## Conclusion

AI has the potential to revolutionize performance evaluation and training, providing organizations with objective and data-driven insights that can drive employee development and business success. However, it is important for organizations to be aware of the potential challenges and limitations of AI and to implement these technologies responsibly and ethically.

# V.IV Case studies of companies successfully implementing AI in human resources

AI is revolutionizing the way human resources (HR) departments operate, and many companies are already seeing the benefits. In this section, we will explore some examples of companies that have successfully implemented AI in HR.

## 1. Hilton Worldwide - Recruitment using AI chatbots

Hilton Worldwide uses an AI chatbot to help with recruitment. The chatbot, named Connie, uses natural language processing to answer candidates' questions about Hilton, the job requirements, and the application process. Connie can also recommend jobs to candidates based on their skills and experience. Hilton has reported that using Connie has reduced the time it takes to fill a position by 90%.

## 2. IBM - Employee engagement using AI

IBM has implemented an AI-powered tool called "Watson Candidate Assistant" that helps employees find internal job opportunities that match their skills and experience. The tool also provides personalized career advice and learning opportunities to help employees advance their careers. IBM has reported that the tool has increased employee engagement and retention.

## 3. Unilever - Diversity and inclusion using AI

Unilever has implemented an AI-powered tool called "Textio" to help with its diversity and inclusion efforts. Textio analyzes job postings and suggests changes to make them more inclusive and attractive to diverse candidates. Unilever has reported that using Textio has resulted in a 23% increase in the number of female candidates and a 58% increase in the number of candidates from diverse backgrounds.

## 4. Hilton Worldwide - Performance evaluation using AI

Hilton Worldwide has also implemented an AI-powered tool for performance evaluation. The tool, called "Elevate", uses AI to analyze employee performance data and provide personalized feedback and recommendations for improvement. Hilton has reported that using Elevate has resulted in a 50% reduction in the time it takes to complete a performance evaluation.

## 5. Intel - Training using AI

Intel has implemented an AI-powered tool called "Intel Insight Platform" to help with employee training. The platform uses AI to analyze employee performance data and identify knowledge gaps. It then provides personalized training recommendations to fill those gaps. Intel has reported that using the platform has resulted in a 50% reduction in the time it takes employees to gain new skills.

These are just a few examples of companies successfully implementing AI in HR. As AI technology continues to evolve, we can expect to see more companies adopt AI-powered tools to improve their HR operations and employee engagement.

# CHAPTER VI:
# ETHICAL AND LEGAL CONSIDERATIONS FOR AI IN BUSINESS

## *VI.I The ethical and legal implications of AI in business*

A rtificial intelligence (AI) is transforming the business world, offering new opportunities to increase efficiency, improve customer experience, and boost profitability. However, as AI becomes more widespread, it also raises important ethical and legal questions that businesses must consider.

One of the main ethical concerns around AI is the potential for bias and discrimination. AI algorithms are only as good as the data they are trained on, and if that data is biased or discriminatory, the algorithm will reproduce those biases. For example, if an AI system is trained on historical hiring data that reflects past discriminatory hiring practices, it may continue to perpetuate those biases in future hiring decisions.

Another ethical concern is the impact of AI on employment. As AI systems become more advanced, they may replace human workers in certain jobs, leading to unemployment and social inequality. Businesses need to consider the ethical implications of AI in their workforce planning and ensure that any job displacement is managed responsibly.

The use of AI also raises important legal questions about data privacy and security. As businesses collect and analyze large amounts of data to train their AI systems, they must ensure that they are doing so in compliance with relevant data protection laws. This includes obtaining the necessary consent from individuals and taking appropriate measures to protect that data from unauthorized access or misuse.

**Additionally**, businesses using AI must also consider liability and responsibility for any negative outcomes resulting from the use of AI systems. For example, if an AI system makes a decision that harms a customer or employee, who is responsible for that decision? This is an important legal question that is still being debated and will likely continue to evolve as AI becomes more prevalent in business.

**In summary**, while AI offers many benefits for businesses, it also raises important ethical and legal questions that must be carefully considered. As AI continues to evolve and become more widespread, businesses need to be proactive in addressing these issues and ensuring that their use of AI is both ethical and legal.

## *VI.II Best practices for ethical and responsible use of AI in business*

As artificial intelligence (AI) continues to revolutionize various industries, businesses need to adopt ethical and responsible practices when implementing AI technologies. The potential benefits of AI are numerous, but they must be balanced against potential ethical and legal implications. In this section, we will discuss some best practices for the ethical and responsible use of AI in business.

1. Start with a clear understanding of the problem: Before implementing AI, it is important to define the problem you want to solve or the opportunity you want to capture. This will help you avoid unintended consequences and ethical issues that may arise from the misuse of AI. Additionally, it is important to engage stakeholders, including employees, customers, and partners, in the development and deployment of AI.
2. Use diverse data sets: To ensure that AI algorithms are unbiased, it is important to use diverse data sets that are representative of the population. This will help mitigate the risk of perpetuating biases or discrimination that may be present in the data.
3. Monitor and evaluate the impact of AI: Once AI is implemented, it is important to continuously monitor and evaluate its impact. This includes assessing the effectiveness of AI in achieving its intended goals and identifying unintended consequences or ethical issues that may arise.
4. Ensure transparency: AI algorithms can be opaque and difficult to understand. It is important to ensure transparency in the development and deployment of AI, including providing explanations of how the algorithms

work and how they make decisions. This will help build trust and accountability with stakeholders.

5. Address privacy and security concerns: As AI involves the use of large amounts of data, it is important to ensure that privacy and security concerns are addressed. This includes implementing appropriate security measures to protect data and ensuring that data is collected, processed, and used in compliance with applicable laws and regulations.

6. Foster an ethical culture: Implementing AI requires a culture of ethics and responsibility. It is important to establish clear ethical guidelines and codes of conduct that guide the development and deployment of AI. Additionally, it is important to provide employees with training and resources to help them understand the ethical and legal implications of AI.

**In conclusion**, AI has the potential to bring significant benefits to businesses, but it must be used ethically and responsibly. By following these best practices, businesses can mitigate the risks of unintended consequences and ensure that AI is used for the benefit of all stakeholders.

## VI.III The regulatory landscape
for AI in business

Artificial intelligence (AI) is transforming the business landscape in many ways, but it also raises important ethical, legal, and regulatory questions. Governments around the world are grappling with how to regulate the use of AI, especially in industries such as finance, healthcare, and transportation, where it has the potential to significantly impact people's lives.

The regulatory landscape for AI in business is still evolving, but several key developments are worth noting. In this section, we'll explore some of these developments and what they mean for businesses using AI.

**Regulatory Approaches to AI**

There are several different approaches to regulating AI in business, ranging from voluntary guidelines to mandatory regulations. Here are a few examples:

- **Voluntary guidelines:** Many industry groups and governments have issued voluntary guidelines for the use of AI in business. These guidelines are designed to promote the ethical and responsible use of AI, but they are not legally binding.

- **Industry-specific regulations:** Some industries, such as healthcare and finance, have specific regulations that govern the use of AI. For example, in the United States, the Food and Drug Administration (FDA) regulates medical devices that use AI.

- **General regulations:** Some governments are considering broader regulations that apply to all businesses using AI. For example, the European Union's

General Data Protection Regulation (GDPR) applies to any business that collects and processes personal data, regardless of whether AI is used.

## Key Regulatory Issues

There are several key regulatory issues that businesses using AI should be aware of:

- **Data privacy:** AI relies on large amounts of data to make decisions, and businesses need to ensure that they are collecting, storing, and processing that data in a way that complies with data privacy regulations.

- **Transparency:** As AI becomes more sophisticated, it can be difficult to understand how it is making decisions. Businesses need to be transparent about how they are using AI and ensure that it is explainable to stakeholders.

- **Bias and discrimination:** AI systems can perpetuate biases and discrimination, especially if they are trained on biased data sets. Businesses need to be aware of these issues and take steps to mitigate them.

- **Liability:** As AI becomes more autonomous, there are questions about who is responsible if something goes wrong. For example, if a self-driving car causes an accident, is the car manufacturer liable, or is the AI system itself responsible?

## Best Practices for Compliance

To comply with the regulations governing AI in business, there are several best practices that businesses should follow:

- **Conduct a risk assessment:** Before implementing AI, businesses should conduct a risk assessment to identify potential risks and develop strategies to mitigate them.

- **Design for transparency and explainability:** Businesses should design AI systems that are transparent and explainable so that stakeholders can understand how decisions are being made.

- **Monitor for bias and discrimination:** Businesses should monitor their AI systems for biases and discrimination and take steps to address them if they are detected.

- **Provide training and support:** Businesses should provide training and support to employees who are working with AI systems, to ensure that they understand how to use them effectively and responsibly.

## Conclusion

As AI continues to transform the business landscape, governments are grappling with how to regulate its use. Businesses that are using AI need to be aware of the regulatory landscape and ensure that they are complying with relevant regulations. By following best practices for the ethical and responsible use of AI, businesses can help to mitigate risks and build trust with stakeholders.

## VI.IV Case studies of companies facing ethical and legal challenges related to AI

Artificial intelligence (AI) is revolutionizing various industries and changing the way we live and work. However, with great power comes great responsibility, and AI is no exception. While AI has the potential to create enormous benefits for businesses and society, it also raises ethical and legal concerns that must be addressed.

In this section, we will explore some case studies of companies that have faced ethical and legal challenges related to AI.

### 1. Amazon's Biased Recruitment Tool

In 2018, it was revealed that Amazon had developed a recruitment tool that used AI to screen resumes and identify the most suitable candidates for the job. However, the system was found to be biased against women, as it had been trained on resumes submitted over the past 10 years, which were predominantly from men. As a result, the system downgraded resumes that contained words commonly used by women, such as "women's" and "feminine." Amazon subsequently abandoned the tool and pledged to improve its recruitment practices.

This case highlights the importance of ensuring that AI systems are trained on diverse data sets and regularly monitored for bias.

### 2. Volkswagen's Emissions Scandal

In 2015, Volkswagen was caught cheating on emissions tests for its diesel cars. The company had installed software that could detect when the car was being tested and reduce emissions to meet the standards. However, in normal driving conditions, the emissions were much higher than the legal limit. The scandal cost

Volkswagen billions of dollars in fines and damages and tarnished its reputation.

This case illustrates the risks of using AI to cheat or deceive and the need for transparency and accountability in AI systems.

### 3. Google's Facial Recognition Tool

In 2021, Google faced criticism over a facial recognition tool it had developed for internal use. The tool was used to tag photos of employees and enable searches based on their faces. However, it was found to be biased against people of color and women, as it had been trained on a data set that was predominantly white and male. Google subsequently suspended the tool and apologized for the harm caused.

This case highlights the need for transparency and oversight in the development and deployment of AI systems, as well as the importance of diversity in AI teams.

### 4. Uber's Self-Driving Car Accident

In 2018, an Uber self-driving car struck and killed a pedestrian in Arizona. The car was in autonomous mode at the time of the accident, but the human backup driver was distracted and failed to intervene. The accident raised questions about the safety of self-driving cars and the responsibility of companies that develop and deploy them.

This case underscores the need for rigorous testing and safety standards for AI systems, and the importance of human oversight and accountability.

## Conclusion

These case studies demonstrate the potential risks and challenges of using AI in business, and the need for ethical and responsible practices to mitigate them. While AI has the potential to create enormous benefits for businesses and society, it must be developed and deployed with caution and care, and with a deep understanding of its ethical and legal implications.

# CHAPTER VII: FUTURE OF AI IN BUSINESS

# VII.I Emerging trends and technologies in AI for business

A rtificial intelligence (AI) has come a long way since its inception and is now being widely used in various industries, including business. AI technologies such as machine learning, natural language processing, and computer vision are increasingly being used by companies to automate and optimize their processes, improve customer experience, and gain insights into their operations.

**Here are some emerging trends and technologies in AI for business:**

1. Edge AI: Edge AI refers to the use of AI on devices located at the edge of the network, such as sensors, smartphones, and other IoT devices. Edge AI can process data in real time and make quick decisions, which is especially useful in industries such as healthcare, manufacturing, and retail.

2. Explainable AI: Explainable AI (XAI) is an emerging field of AI that aims to create transparent and interpretable AI systems. XAI is important because it can help businesses avoid biased decisions and improve accountability.

3. AI-powered cybersecurity: AI can help businesses improve their cybersecurity by detecting and responding to threats in real time. AI can also help businesses automate routine cybersecurity tasks, such as patching and updating software.

4. Autonomous systems: Autonomous systems refer to systems that can operate without human intervention. Autonomous systems are being used in industries such as transportation, logistics, and manufacturing to improve

efficiency and reduce costs.

5. AI and blockchain: AI and blockchain are two technologies that are being combined to create new business models and applications. For example, blockchain can be used to create a decentralized AI marketplace, where companies can buy and sell AI models and data.

6. Quantum computing: Quantum computing is an emerging technology that has the potential to revolutionize AI. Quantum computing can solve complex optimization problems that are currently impossible for classical computers to solve, which can lead to breakthroughs in areas such as drug discovery and logistics optimization.

**In conclusion**, AI is an ever-evolving field, and businesses must keep up with the latest trends and technologies to stay ahead of the competition. By leveraging these emerging AI technologies, businesses can gain a competitive advantage and unlock new opportunities for growth and innovation.

## VII.II Predictions for the future of AI in business

Artificial intelligence (AI) has already begun to transform the business world, but many experts believe that we have only scratched the surface of what this technology can achieve. As AI becomes more sophisticated and more widely adopted, it is likely to have an even greater impact on how businesses operate and compete in the future. Here are some predictions for what we can expect from AI in business in the years to come.

1. Increased automation: One of the most significant ways that AI is likely to change business is through increased automation. As AI algorithms become more advanced and capable, they will be able to perform a wider range of tasks that currently require human intervention. This will lead to greater efficiency and lower costs for businesses, but it may also result in job losses for some workers.

2. Personalization at scale: As AI systems become better at analyzing data and understanding human behavior, they will be able to deliver more personalized experiences to customers at scale. This could include everything from personalized marketing messages to customized product recommendations.

3. More intelligent chatbots: Chatbots are already being used by many businesses to provide basic customer support, but as AI technology advances, these bots will become more intelligent and capable of handling more complex tasks. This could include everything from booking appointments to troubleshooting technical issues.

4. Enhanced cybersecurity: As businesses become more reliant on AI and other digital technologies, cybersecurity threats will become more sophisticated and harder to

detect. However, AI can also be used to improve cybersecurity by analyzing vast amounts of data and identifying patterns that indicate potential threats.

5. Greater use of predictive analytics: Predictive analytics is already being used by many businesses to forecast future trends and make better decisions, but as AI technology advances, these systems will become even more accurate and powerful. This could lead to more accurate sales forecasts, improved supply chain management, and better risk management.

6. Integration with blockchain technology: Blockchain technology has already begun to transform industries such as finance and logistics, and AI is likely to play an increasingly important role in these applications. AI algorithms can be used to analyze blockchain data and identify patterns that could be used to optimize supply chain management or prevent fraud.

7. More advanced natural language processing: Natural language processing (NLP) is already being used by many businesses to analyze customer feedback and social media posts, but as AI technology advances, these systems will become more sophisticated and capable of handling more complex tasks. This could include everything from analyzing legal documents to understanding the nuances of human conversation.

8. Continued ethical and regulatory challenges: As AI technology continues to evolve, it will pose new ethical and regulatory challenges for businesses. It will be important for companies to prioritize ethical considerations and ensure that their AI systems are transparent and accountable.

9. Greater collaboration between humans and machines: While some fear that AI will replace human workers, many experts believe that the future of work will involve greater collaboration between humans and machines. As AI systems become more sophisticated, they will be able to

take on more routine tasks, freeing up humans to focus on more creative and strategic work.

10. New and unexpected applications: Finally, as AI technology continues to advance, we are likely to see new and unexpected applications of this technology in the business world. From healthcare to education to agriculture, there are countless ways that AI could be used to improve efficiency, productivity, and outcomes in a wide range of industries.

**In conclusion**, the future of AI in business is likely to be both exciting and challenging. As this technology continues to evolve and mature, it will be important for businesses to stay abreast of the latest developments and adapt their strategies accordingly. By embracing AI responsibly and ethically, businesses can unlock new opportunities and gain a competitive edge in the years to come.

## *VII.III Implications of AI for the workforce and society*

Artificial intelligence (AI) has been transforming the world of business, enabling organizations to automate processes, gain insights, and make informed decisions. While AI has the potential to bring numerous benefits to businesses, it also raises concerns about its impact on the workforce and society as a whole.

One of the main implications of AI for the workforce is the displacement of jobs. As AI and automation continue to advance, many traditional jobs may become obsolete or significantly reduced in demand. For example, routine manual labor jobs, such as assembly line work or data entry, can now be performed by robots and AI algorithms.

**However**, the same technologies that are displacing jobs can also create new ones. AI is creating demand for workers with skills such as data analysis, machine learning, and programming. In fact, according to a report by the World Economic Forum, AI is expected to create 2.3 million new jobs by 2025.

AI also has implications for the way work is performed. With the rise of remote work and virtual collaboration, AI-powered tools can help to facilitate communication, collaboration, and productivity across geographically dispersed teams. AI algorithms can also be used to monitor employee performance and provide real-time feedback, potentially enhancing productivity and efficiency.

**However**, there are also concerns about the potential misuse of AI-powered monitoring tools. Employers may use these tools to collect and analyze data on employees without their knowledge or consent, leading to issues of privacy and surveillance.

AI also has broader societal implications, particularly around issues of bias and fairness. AI algorithms are only as unbiased as the data they are trained on, and if the data is biased, the algorithm's outputs will be biased as well. This can lead to perpetuating existing inequalities and discrimination.

To address these concerns, businesses, and policymakers need to develop ethical and responsible frameworks for the development and deployment of AI technologies. This includes ensuring transparency in AI decision-making processes, implementing safeguards to protect against bias and discrimination, and providing opportunities for reskilling and upskilling workers whose jobs are displaced by automation.

**In conclusion**, AI has the potential to bring significant benefits to businesses, but it also raises important ethical and societal implications. It is up to businesses and policymakers to work together to ensure that AI is developed and deployed responsibly and ethically, to minimize its negative impacts and maximize its potential for positive change.

## VII.IV Opportunities and challenges for businesses in the AI era

Artificial intelligence (AI) is rapidly transforming the way businesses operate, with its potential to enhance efficiency, increase productivity, and enable new services and products. However, with the opportunities come challenges and risks, such as the need for new skills, the ethical implications of AI, and concerns about job displacement. In this section, we will discuss the opportunities and challenges that businesses face in the AI era.

**Opportunities:**

1. Enhanced Efficiency: AI can automate routine tasks, reducing the workload for employees and increasing productivity. It can also optimize processes and enable more accurate decision-making.
2. Improved Customer Experience: AI can personalize products and services to the needs of individual customers, enhancing their experience and satisfaction.
3. New Revenue Streams: AI can enable new services and products, creating new revenue streams for businesses. For example, AI-powered chatbots can offer 24/7 customer support or AI-powered medical diagnostics can improve patient outcomes.
4. Competitive Advantage: AI can provide businesses with a competitive edge by enabling them to quickly respond to changing market conditions, reducing costs, and improving customer experience.

**Challenges:**

1. The Need for New Skills: The implementation of AI in business requires new skills, including data analysis,

machine learning, and programming. Businesses need to invest in training and development to ensure their workforce is equipped with the necessary skills.

2. Ethical Implications: AI raises ethical concerns related to privacy, bias, and transparency. Businesses need to develop ethical guidelines and frameworks to ensure the responsible and transparent use of AI.

3. Job Displacement: The implementation of AI could lead to job displacement as routine tasks become automated. However, businesses can mitigate this by reskilling employees for new roles that require human skills, such as creativity and problem-solving.

4. Security Risks: AI systems are vulnerable to cyber threats and attacks. Businesses need to invest in cybersecurity to protect their systems and data from unauthorized access.

**In conclusion**, the opportunities and challenges presented by AI for businesses are significant. While there are risks and challenges, the benefits of AI outweigh the potential downsides. Businesses that adopt AI responsibly and invest in their workforce will be better positioned to take advantage of the opportunities presented by the AI era.

# CHAPTER VIII: SUMMARY

# VIII.I Summary

"AI in Business: Real-World Case Studies and Applications" is a comprehensive guide to the transformative potential of artificial intelligence in the business world. The book explores real-world case studies and applications of AI across different business domains, examining the benefits and challenges associated with the technology.

The book covers a range of topics, including optimizing operations, improving decision-making, creating new sources of value for customers and stakeholders, and ethical and legal considerations. Through examining these topics, readers gain insights into the potential of AI to revolutionize business operations, as well as the challenges and limitations of the technology.

Throughout the book, readers will learn from the successes and challenges of companies that have implemented AI, and gain a better understanding of the opportunities and risks associated with this technology. The book also provides practical guidance for business leaders and professionals on how to implement AI responsibly and ethically.

Overall, "AI in Business: Real-World Case Studies and Applications" provides a comprehensive and insightful overview of AI in the business world, and is a valuable resource for anyone interested in the transformative potential of this exciting technology.

# CHAPTER IX: CONCLUSION AND TAKEAWAYS

# IX.I Recap of the key themes and insights from the book

"Artificial Intelligence (AI) in Business: Real-World Case Studies and Applications" explores how artificial intelligence (AI) is transforming the way businesses operate across a range of industries, including marketing, sales, operations, finance, human resources, and more. The book highlights the potential benefits and challenges of AI adoption, with real-world case studies and examples of successful implementations.

One of the key themes of the book is the importance of data in AI applications. By collecting and analyzing large volumes of data, businesses can use AI to gain insights and make better decisions. This can help companies optimize their operations, improve their products and services, and ultimately drive growth and profitability.

Another theme is the role of AI in improving customer experiences. By using AI-powered chatbots and virtual assistants, businesses can provide personalized and responsive support to customers, improving satisfaction and loyalty. AI can also be used for market research and customer segmentation, allowing companies to identify and target the most valuable customers.

**In addition**, the book explores the potential of AI for optimizing production and logistics, through predictive maintenance and quality control, as well as supply chain management using blockchain technology. AI can also be used for financial reporting and compliance, credit scoring and underwriting, and recruitment and talent management.

**However**, the book also highlights the ethical and legal implications of AI adoption, including concerns around privacy, bias, and job displacement. It offers best practices for the responsible and ethical use of AI in business, as well as an overview of the regulatory landscape for AI.

**Overall**, "AI in Business: Real-World Case Studies and Applications" provides a comprehensive overview of the opportunities and challenges of AI for businesses today. It offers insights and examples of successful AI implementations, as well as a roadmap for the ethical and responsible adoption of AI.

## IX.II Recommendations for businesses looking to implement AI

Artificial intelligence (AI) is rapidly transforming the business world, offering opportunities for companies to improve efficiency, reduce costs, and enhance customer experiences. However, implementing AI is not without its challenges. Here are some recommendations for businesses looking to implement AI:

1. Start with a clear strategy: Before implementing AI, it's important to identify your business goals and determine how AI can help achieve them. This will help you focus on the areas where AI can have the greatest impact.

2. Build a strong data foundation: AI relies on data, so it's essential to ensure that your data is accurate, complete, and relevant. This includes data from internal sources as well as external sources such as social media and customer feedback.

3. Choose the right technology and partners: There are many different AI technologies and platforms available, so it's important to choose the ones that are best suited to your business needs. It's also important to work with partners who have the necessary expertise and experience to help you implement AI successfully.

4. Prioritize ethical considerations: AI raises ethical and social issues that need to be addressed. Businesses should prioritize ethical considerations and ensure that AI is used responsibly and transparently.

5. Foster a culture of innovation: Implementing AI requires a culture of innovation and experimentation. Companies should encourage employees to explore new ideas and technologies and provide resources and support to help them do so.

6. Invest in employee training: AI will change the nature of work and require new skills and competencies. Companies should invest in employee training and development to ensure that their workforce is equipped to work with AI effectively.

Implementing AI can be challenging, but with the right strategy, technology, and culture, it can offer significant benefits for businesses. By prioritizing ethical considerations, investing in employee training, and fostering a culture of innovation, businesses can stay ahead of the curve and reap the rewards of the AI era.

## VIII.III Implications of AI for the broader society and economy.

Artificial Intelligence (AI) has come a long way in recent years, and its impact is being felt across many different sectors of society and the economy. While AI has the potential to bring significant benefits, such as improved efficiency, productivity, and innovation, it also presents some significant challenges that need to be addressed. In this section, we will explore some of the implications of AI for the broader society and economy.

One of the most significant implications of AI is its potential to disrupt employment. As machines become more capable of performing tasks that were previously only possible for humans, there is a real risk that many jobs will be replaced by automation. This has the potential to cause significant social and economic upheaval, as large numbers of people find themselves out of work. While some experts argue that new jobs will be created to replace those lost to automation, others believe that the pace of change may be too rapid for many workers to keep up.

Another significant implication of AI is its potential impact on income inequality. As AI becomes more prevalent, likely, those with the skills and knowledge to work with these technologies will be in high demand, while those without these skills may struggle to find meaningful employment. This could exacerbate existing inequalities, both within and between countries.

AI also raises important questions about privacy and data security. As more and more data is collected and analyzed by AI systems, there is a risk that this information could be used for nefarious purposes, such as identity theft or corporate espionage. Additionally, AI systems may be vulnerable to cyber-attacks or other forms of hacking, which could compromise the integrity of the data they rely on.

**Finally**, AI raises important ethical questions about the role of machines in society. As machines become more capable of making decisions that were previously the domain of humans, it is important to consider the ethical implications of these decisions. For example, how do we ensure that machines make decisions that are fair and unbiased, and that reflect our values as a society?

**In conclusion**, AI has the potential to bring significant benefits to society and the economy, but it also presents some significant challenges that need to be addressed. As we move forward into an increasingly AI-driven world, it is essential that we carefully consider the implications of these technologies and work to mitigate their negative impacts. By doing so, we can ensure that AI is used in a way that benefits us all.

# EPILOGUE

As we come to the end of our exploration of AI in business, I hope that this book has provided valuable insights and perspectives on the transformative potential of this exciting technology. We have examined real-world case studies and applications of AI across different business domains, and we have explored the challenges and limitations of AI, including ethical and legal considerations.

We have seen that AI has the potential to revolutionize the way businesses operate and compete in the global marketplace. By leveraging the power of AI, businesses can optimize their operations, improve decision-making, and create new sources of value for customers and stakeholders. However, we have also seen that the key to success with AI is not just in the technology itself, but in how businesses use it to create value for their stakeholders.

As we look to the future, it is clear that AI will continue to play an increasingly important role in the business world. Emerging technologies such as deep learning, natural language generation, and edge computing are enabling new applications of AI, and businesses that can leverage these technologies effectively will gain a competitive advantage in the marketplace.

However, as with any transformative technology, there are also risks and challenges associated with AI. Ethical considerations, such as privacy and bias, must be carefully navigated, and businesses must be proactive in addressing these issues. Additionally, the pace of technological change means that businesses must be agile and adaptable to stay ahead of the curve.

As I close this book, I encourage business leaders and professionals to approach the opportunities and challenges of AI with an open mind and a willingness to learn. By continuing to explore the potential of AI, we can unlock new sources of innovation and value for our organizations and society as a whole.

Thank you for joining me on this journey into the world of AI in business, and I wish you the best of luck in your future endeavors.

# AFTERWORD

As we reflect on the insights and perspectives shared throughout this book, it is clear that AI has the potential to transform the way businesses operate and compete in the global marketplace. From optimizing operations and improving decision-making to creating new sources of value for customers and stakeholders, AI has the power to drive innovation and growth across all sectors of the economy.

However, as we have seen, realizing the full potential of AI requires more than just the technology itself. It requires a holistic approach that takes into account the unique needs and challenges of each business domain, as well as the ethical and legal considerations associated with AI.

I hope that this book has provided a comprehensive guide to AI in business, based on real-world case studies and applications. By learning from the successes and challenges of companies that have implemented AI, I hope that business leaders and professionals will be better equipped to navigate the opportunities and challenges of this exciting technology.

I also hope that this book has sparked a broader conversation about the role of AI in society and the need for responsible and ethical AI development. As AI continues to transform the way we live and work, we must approach its development and deployment with a deep commitment to ethical principles such as fairness, transparency, and accountability.

I thank you for joining me on this journey into the world of AI in business, and I invite you to continue exploring the potential of this transformative technology. Together, we can create a future where AI is used to improve the lives of people and the health of our planet.

# ABOUT THE AUTHOR

## Moustafa Elgezery

As a Linux expert, data scientist, machine learning engineer, and author, I'm passionate about using technology to solve complex problems and drive innovation. With over ten years of experience in the industry, I have honed my skills in areas such as Linux administration, IT automation, Scripting, Data preprocessing, and analysis, interpreting data to help drive decision-making, and researching, building, and designing self-running artificial intelligence (AI) systems to automate predictive models.

I prioritize integrity, excellence, innovation, collaboration, and impact. I strive to stay up-to-date with the latest developments in my field.

As an author, I believe sharing knowledge is crucial to advancing this field and enabling others to succeed. I dedicate myself to using my skills and expertise to achieve a positive impact worldwide, and I am excited to continue growing and learning in my work.

# THANK YOU!

www.ingramcontent.com/pod-product-compliance
Lightning Source LLC
Chambersburg PA
CBHW070403220526
45467CB00001B/472